911

PSALM

A Call for Goodness, Mercy,
Deliverance and Restoration

AHMES ASKIA, PhD

BALBOA.
PRESS

A DIVISION OF HAY HOUSE

Balboa Press books may be ordered through booksellers or by contacting:

Balboa Press
A Division of Hay House
1663 Liberty Drive
Bloomington, IN 47403
www.balboapress.com
1 (877) 407-4847

Print information available on the last page.

ISBN: 978-1-9822-2531-5 (sc)
ISBN: 978-1-9822-2533-9 (hc)
ISBN: 978-1-9822-2532-2 (e)

Library of Congress Control Number: 2019903941

Balboa Press rev. date: 04/05/2019

Introduction

Several years ago I was speaking with my pastor and he suggested that I read the entire 119th number of the Psalms. He told me few people are able to see the beauty in this Psalm because it is not only the longest Psalm, but also the longest verse in the Bible. I consider myself an avid reader so this piqued my interest.

To my utter surprise I immediately encountered each section as a unique personality; a teacher and then after many months, a friend. Each morning I would rush to my place of meditation and greet them with "good morning guys."

I kept reading the entire 119th number of the Psalm every morning and before long, three years had passed. Somewhere along the way each section became a meditation for me. Oh, how I love these guys.

When I told my pastor that I had been reading the entire Psalm for three years, he was amazed, so full was my joy in relating how much I love it, or as I told him, how much I love them; each "person" of Psalm 119. He patiently reminded me that each section is a letter of the Hebrew alphabet.

Regardless, for me, each is a trusted friend whom I have grown to love a great deal. I miss them a lot when, because of my schedule, I don't read all of them in one sitting.

Each reminds us that we have goodness, mercy, deliverance, and restoration in the Holy Spirit and we have only to say what Christ says.

We learn, among so much more, two life-changing lessons after Jesus' 40-day fast. Read the entire account in Luke 4:1-12.

The first lesson for us is that contrary thoughts have no sense of time. We should use that to our advantage.

Jesus ends 40 days of fasting; communing with the Father. A tempter thought comes to speak to Him. Jesus is incredibly strong after His fast. He has communed with God forty days and nights. Timing!!!

So when the tempter thought of, "If you be the Christ...," comes to him, Jesus answers with, "It Is written."

Even though the next tempter thought tries to use God's Word against Jesus by saying "It is written..." Jesus responds, "It is also written..."

This should be our response to every contrary thought who speaks to us. "It is written."

Needless to say, we will need to study and know the Word of God in order to be able to declare the Word of God, even and especially, when it is used against us.

The second crucial lesson is this; Jesus' example for us is that the Word defeats the thought.

Truly, if you don't go any further than this point you will walk in victory. Don't just *think* about what the Word of God says, open your mouth and speak aloud to that thought, "It is written."

As believers in Christ each of us has victory in our own life nestled in Jesus' life, His death, and His resurrection.

I wrestled with how to classify this work…a day planner, a journal, a devotional. For me, it's all three in one.

911 Psalm is not an interpretation of the scriptures. It is a call in devotion to the Holy Spirit for help. It is a call to journal our day with the Holy Spirit's help. It is a call to plan our day with guidance from the Holy Spirit. Like any 911 call, the purpose gets the help you need. Like any 911 call, urgency drives the moment. Like any 911 call, the need is personal and can often involve someone or something outside of one's self. And yes, like any 911 call, you are calling the person you believe you can rely on to give you immediate and absolute help.

It is written, "God is our refuge and our strength, a very present help in trouble."

Use the 911 call pages following each section to call out your greatest needs in the Holy Spirit.

Some days, you might feel the need for goodness—a clean heart, mercy—relief from thoughts of sorrow and worry, deliverance—cradled from thoughts of doubt or isolation, and restoration—fullness of joy and the Holy Spirit.

Other times the need is more focused on only one and not so much on all.

Make the call. Use the 911 call pages for what works best for your life on your journey.

If I have learned nothing else from my friends in the verses of Psalm 119 it is that thoughts can be very powerful but they cower at the Word of God.

We have a response to thoughts of sorrow, worry, lack, and pain. It is written, "He was bruised for our iniquity, the chastisement of His peace is upon us and with His strips we are healed."

We have a response to thoughts of doubt. It is written, "I can do all things through Christ who strengthens me."

We have a response for thoughts of isolation. If you can just remember that being lonesome is not the same as being alone and being alone need not be the same as being lonesome. It is written, "I will never leave you or forsake you."

The Word of God defeats the thought.

We have a response for every thought contrary to victory in Christ…"It is written."

Command yourself daily to be inquisitive, to hunger and thirst to know what God says, to know the Word of God so that you can declare it.

The scripture challenges us in Proverbs 28:1, "The wicked man flees, though no one pursues, but the righteous are as bold as a lion."

We must boldly call for Goodness, Mercy, Deliverance, and Restoration in Christ. Because He told us in His Word that greater works shall we do; He has sent us the Comforter, the Holy Spirit. We can speak boldly with reliance on the Lord!

Surely, if contrary thoughts are audacious enough to confront us, we must be even more audacious, stand firm and open our mouth and scream, if we have to, as we declare the Word of God.

As God promised to Abraham in Genesis 15:1, so He says to us today. "Do not be afraid, I am your shield, your exceedingly great reward."

Reading the entire 119th number of the Psalms daily has enriched my daily walk with the Lord in a myriad of ways. It truly gives a peace that passes all understanding.

My prayer is to be like the disciples of the early church, to be continually filled with joy and the Holy Spirit. I want to be an adherent who makes the Word of God the rule of conduct for my life.

Grace to you and peace be multiplied.

Aleph

Victorious and pure in heart are all
who walk in the way of Christ Jesus
our Lord,
Who walk in faith in the Lord!
Victorious in every way are those
who search for His victories;
who search for Him with all of their
being and with everything that is
within them!
They also reject contrary thoughts,
especially thoughts of doubt and isolation.
They walk in His way.
You, O Lord, have commanded us
to diligently walk in grace and truth.
Direct my way to say what You say!
Then I will not be ashamed
when I walk on Your path.

I praise you with all I have within me
as I learn Your righteous Word.
I keep saying what You say.
Your Word says, "I will never leave you or
forsake you."
I declare the Lord will never leave me or
forsake me. Your Word says, "I am with
you always even until the end of the world."
I declare, the Lord is with me forever
and ever throughout eternity.
I am not forsaken!

911 What Is Your Emergency?

Holy Spirit, today, right now I need...

_____

_____

_____

_____

_____

_____

_____

_____

_____

_____

_____

_____

_____

_____

_____

_____

_____

I Trust You Lord!

911 What Is Your Emergency?

Holy Spirit, today, right now I need...

_____

_____

_____

_____

_____

_____

_____

_____

_____

_____

_____

_____

_____

_____

_____

_____

_____

I Trust You Lord!

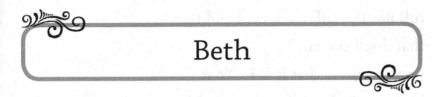

Beth

How can I see my way?
By following in Your Holy Spirit, by
obeying You.
With my whole being I seek You. Oh
let me not wander from Your path.
Your Holy Spirit is in my heart,
that I not sin against You.
How can I help but sing and shout!
Victorious are You, O Lord! Teach me
to say what You say.
With my mouth I declare the Word
of Your mouth.
I rejoice in just the thought of your
victories as much as in all riches.
I meditate on Your grace and truth,
and I study Your way.
I guide and remind myself to say

what You say;
I do not forget Your Word.
"The earth is the Lord's and the
fullness thereof, the world and they
that dwell therein."
Lord, I rejoice that it is in Your
Holy Spirit that I live, I move, I have my being.

911 What Is Your Emergency?

Holy Spirit, today, right now I need...

_____

_____

_____

_____

_____

_____

_____

_____

_____

_____

_____

_____

_____

_____

_____

_____

I Trust You Lord!

911 What Is Your Emergency?

Holy Spirit, today, right now I need...

_____

_____

_____

_____

_____

_____

_____

_____

_____

_____

_____

_____

_____

_____

_____

_____

_____

_____

I Trust You Lord!

Gimel

Deal bountifully with me Lord,
that I live and keep Your Word.
Open my eyes so that I see
Wondrous things that are evident
when walking by faith in You.
Open to me the gates of righteousness.
Save me, grant me success, send
now prosperity.
Lord, give me the victories that You
have commanded for my life.
They are righteous and very faithful.
My thoughts are a stranger in the earth.
Do not hide Your path from me.
Hold me with Your powerful hand.
Map my way.
My soul weeps with longing
for Your Word at all times.

You rebuke contrary thoughts,
those thoughts who stray from Your path.
Remove me from the path of thoughts
of doubt and isolation
as I move into Your victories.
Thoughts with very little power or
authority speak to me.
But I meditate on saying what You say.
Righteous are You, Lord and righteous
is Your Word.
Your understanding is infinite!
Your victories are my guides.
Your victories, O Lord, are also my counselors.

911 What Is Your Emergency?

Holy Spirit, today, right now I need...

_____

_____

_____

_____

_____

_____

_____

_____

_____

_____

_____

_____

_____

_____

_____

_____

I Trust You Lord!

911 What Is Your Emergency?

Holy Spirit, today, right now I need...

_____

_____

_____

_____

_____

_____

_____

_____

_____

_____

_____

_____

_____

_____

_____

_____

_____

I Trust You Lord!

Daleth

My soul is housed in a physical body.
Breathe into me Lord, restore my soul
according to Your Word.
I want to live in You and You cradle
me back to You.
Teach me to say what You say.
Make me understand the way of
Your grace and truth
so that I meditate on Your wonderful works.
For truly, "I meditate on the glorious
splendor of Your majesty and
on Your wondrous works."
My soul melts from the heaviness
of this physical body.
Strengthen me according to Your Word.
Remove me from the path of thoughts
who are contrary to You, O Lord.

Correct me with grace and mercy.

I walk by faith in Your Word.

I choose the way of truth.

Your Word I lay before me

and I cling to Your victories.

Lord, do not let me be ashamed!

I can run the course of Your path, because You have enlarged my heart.

911 What Is Your Emergency?

Holy Spirit, today, right now I need...

_____

_____

_____

_____

_____

_____

_____

_____

_____

_____

_____

_____

_____

_____

_____

_____

_____

I Trust You Lord!

911 What Is Your Emergency?

Holy Spirit, today, right now I need...

_____

_____

_____

_____

_____

_____

_____

_____

_____

_____

_____

_____

_____

_____

_____

_____

_____

I Trust You Lord!

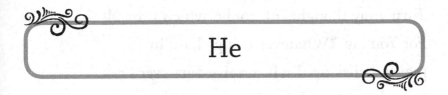

He

Teach me, O Lord, to be bold in
saying what You say,
and I will do so forever and ever
throughout eternity.
Give me understanding so that I
walk in faith.
Indeed, so that I practice faith in all I do,
with all of my being.
Make me walk on the path that
gives me protection through faith in
Your Word.
I am guided on Your path.
Lift my heart to reach for Your
victories and not to covetousness.
Turn my eyes away from desire and
looking at worthless things.
Breathe into me Lord, restore my soul

in Your way.
Establish Your Spirit in me,
who is devoted to obeying You.
Turn away thoughts of doubt, which I dread.
For You say, "Whatever things I ask in
prayer, believing, I will receive whatever I ask."
I proclaim that I have the victories that
God has commanded for my life. They are
righteous and very faithful. Righteous are
You, Lord, and righteous is Your Word.
Truly I long for Your grace and truth
for in them I am safe.
Breathe into me Lord, restore my soul
in Your righteousness.

911 What Is Your Emergency?

Holy Spirit, today, right now I need...

_____

_____

_____

_____

_____

_____

_____

_____

_____

_____

_____

_____

_____

_____

_____

_____

I Trust You Lord!

911 What Is Your Emergency?

Holy Spirit, today, right now I need...

_____

_____

_____

_____

_____

_____

_____

_____

_____

_____

_____

_____

_____

_____

_____

_____

I Trust You Lord!

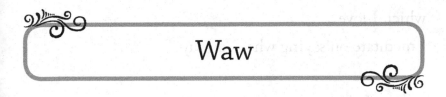

Waw

Lord, let good things come to me
and Your deliverance according to
your Word. Then I have an answer
for all who doubt me.
Lord, I trust Your Holy Spirit.
And take not the Word of truth utterly
out of my mouth.
For I hope in Your design for Heaven and earth.
So I study Your Word,
And have faith in You continually.
Forever and ever throughout eternity.
I walk in liberty,
As I seek Your grace and truth.
I speak of Your victories also to
thoughts who have great power
but no authority.
Therefore, I am not ashamed.

I guide and remind myself to stay on Your path,
which I love.
My hands I lift up on Your path,
which I love.
I meditate on saying what You say.

911 What Is Your Emergency?

Holy Spirit, today, right now I need...

_____

_____

_____

_____

_____

_____

_____

_____

_____

_____

_____

_____

_____

_____

_____

_____

_____

I Trust You Lord!

911 What Is Your Emergency?

Holy Spirit, today, right now I need...

_____

_____

_____

_____

_____

_____

_____

_____

_____

_____

_____

_____

_____

_____

_____

_____

I Trust You Lord!

Zayin

I remember the yes to me,
upon which You caused me to hope.
Your Word makes known, "No matter
how many promises God has made,
they are Yes, in Christ.
And so through Him the Amen is
spoken by us, to the glory of God."
I lock this word in my heart.
This is my comfort, Lord,
when thoughts of sorrow and worry
speak to me;
when I don't see the manifestation.
For Your yes gives me energy.
Contrary thoughts mock me.
Even so, I do not turn away from my
faith in Your Word.
I remember Your word You taught me

years ago, O Lord.
And comfort myself with how they
moved in my life on my behalf.
Thoughts of sorrow and worry
take hold of me,
because I pay attention to them
when I move out of Your protective Word.
"My heart is overflowing with a good theme.
My tongue is the pen of a ready writer."
Saying what You say is my song in
this body You gave me.
It's a melody of love divine.
I remember Your name in the night.
I walk by faith in Your Word.
"I will lie down and sleep in peace
for You alone, O Lord, make me
dwell in safety."
For You alone are God and You are God alone.
Your Word becomes my words
as I walk in grace and truth.

911 What Is Your Emergency?

Holy Spirit, today, right now I need...

_____

_____

_____

_____

_____

_____

_____

_____

_____

_____

_____

_____

_____

_____

_____

_____

I Trust You Lord!

911 What Is Your Emergency?

Holy Spirit, today, right now I need...

_____

_____

_____

_____

_____

_____

_____

_____

_____

_____

_____

_____

_____

_____

_____

_____

_____

I Trust You Lord!

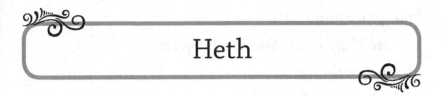

Heth

Lord, I want You to be my whole thought.
I promise to diligently study Your Word.
I beg for Your favor with all of my being;
For You alone are God and You are God alone.
Send goodness and mercy to commune
with me, O God, according to Your Word.
I think about my ways,
and I turn my feet toward Your victories.
I make haste and do not delay to stay on Your path,
which I love.
Wicked thoughts bind me in what
feels like cords.
But I have not forgotten that I walk by faith.
At midnight I rise to give thanks to You.
Because in the silence I can hear
your righteous Word.

Let my thoughts be companion to all thoughts who obey
You Lord.
And those thoughts who mirror and reflect
Your grace and truth.
You are Holy Lord. Your Holy Spirit
fills the earth.
Your glory fills the earth.
Teach me to say what You say.

911 What Is Your Emergency?

Holy Spirit, today, right now I need...

_____

_____

_____

_____

_____

_____

_____

_____

_____

_____

_____

_____

_____

_____

_____

_____

I Trust You Lord!

911 What Is Your Emergency?

Holy Spirit, today, right now I need...

_____

_____

_____

_____

_____

_____

_____

_____

_____

_____

_____

_____

_____

_____

I Trust You Lord!

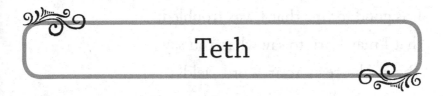

Teth

You have dealt well with me
O Lord, according to Your Word.
You give me victories, which You
have commanded for my life.
Teach me good thinking and knowledge.
Guide me on Your path.
My thoughts were troubled and
I went astray.
But now Lord, I keep Your Word,
I walk in Your power. You, O Lord,
are good and Your Word is truth.
Teach me to say what You say.
Contrary thoughts form lies to
constantly speak to me.
But, with my whole heart,
I hold on to Your grace and truth.
Contrary thoughts are as thick and

clingy as grease.

But I declare that I am guided by

faith in God's Word.

It is good for me that I was troubled;

that I may learn to say what You say.

The guidance of Your Word yields

thousands of coins of gold and silver to me.

Following Your Word makes

me rich and adds no thoughts of sorrow or

worry with it.

911 What Is Your Emergency?

Holy Spirit, today, right now I need...

_____

_____

_____

_____

_____

_____

_____

_____

_____

_____

_____

_____

_____

_____

_____

_____

I Trust You Lord!

911 What Is Your Emergency?

Holy Spirit, today, right now I need...

_____

_____

_____

_____

_____

_____

_____

_____

_____

_____

_____

_____

_____

_____

_____

_____

_____

I Trust You Lord!

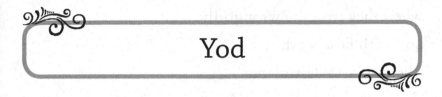

Yod

Lord, Your hand has made me
and fashioned me; please quiet my soul.
Give me understanding, that I may
know Your path, Your way.
And please give me sure footing.
Those who fear You will be glad
when they see me;
because I hope in Your Word.
Lord I know that Your Word is right
and that in my faithlessness
I am troubled.
Let, I pray, living in Your Holy
Spirit be my comfort, according to
Your Word to me.
Let Your Holy Spirit cradle to me
that I may live and experience
Your victories.

Faith in Your Word is my compass
and my guide.
Let contrary thoughts be ashamed
when they treat me wrongfully
and with falsehood.
They work to destroy me;
they try to make an end of me on earth.
But I meditate on Your grace and truth.
Let those thoughts who obey You
speak to me, those thoughts who
know Your victories. Let my heart be
blameless regarding saying what You say;
That I may not be ashamed or shame You.
It is in Your Holy Spirit that I live, I move,
I have my being.

911 What Is Your Emergency?

Holy Spirit, today, right now I need...

_____

_____

_____

_____

_____

_____

_____

_____

_____

_____

_____

_____

_____

_____

_____

_____

_____

I Trust You Lord!

911 What Is Your Emergency?

Holy Spirit, today, right now I need...

_____

_____

_____

_____

_____

_____

_____

_____

_____

_____

_____

_____

_____

_____

_____

_____

I Trust You Lord!

Kaph

My soul waits quietly for Your deliverance,
and I have hope in Your Word.
My soul trembles reaching for Your Word,
saying, "When will You restore me?"
I do not want to become like wineskin
in smoke, worthless!
Lord, I jump and shout and
say what You say.
How many are my days of longing?
When will You magnify Your Word in
me over thoughts who persecute me?
Contrary thoughts have dug pits for me.
Still, my faith is not hampered.
Because I see that Your path is sure and secure.
Wicked thoughts persecute me wrongfully.
Help me!
They try to make an end of me on earth.

They work to destroy me.

Even as I walk in Your grace and truth.

Breathe into me Lord, restore my

soul according to Your lovingkindness,

so that I live and experience the victories

of Your mouth.

911 What Is Your Emergency?

Holy Spirit, today, right now I need...

_____

_____

_____

_____

_____

_____

_____

_____

_____

_____

_____

_____

_____

_____

I Trust You Lord!

911 What Is Your Emergency?

Holy Spirit, today, right now I need...

_____

_____

_____

_____

_____

_____

_____

_____

_____

_____

_____

_____

_____

_____

_____

I Trust You Lord!

Lamed

Forever and ever throughout eternity, Lord,
You declare Your Word to be settled
in Heaven and earth.
Your faithfulness endures to all generations.
You created the universe and gave
man dominion over it.
Everything continues according to
how You designed it;
and all belongs to You.
For You alone are God and You are
God alone.
Without faith in Your Word, as my guide,
I would have perished in my trouble.
I want to always walk in Your grace
and truth.
For by them You have given me life.
O Lord I belong to You, save me.

Grant me success.

Send now prosperity.

Give me the victories that You have
commanded for my life.

They are righteous and very faithful.

I continue to look and listen for Your
grace and truth.

Open to me the gates of righteousness.

Because wicked thoughts wait for
me to destroy me.

They want to make an end of me on earth.

But I pay attention to Your victories.

I see the evidence of all perfection.

The fullness of the evidence of Your Holy
Spirit is exceedingly broad.

I can't help but sing and shout!

911 What Is Your Emergency?

Holy Spirit, today, right now I need...

_____

_____

_____

_____

_____

_____

_____

_____

_____

_____

_____

_____

_____

_____

_____

I Trust You Lord!

911 What Is Your Emergency?

Holy Spirit, today, right now I need...

_____

_____

_____

_____

_____

_____

_____

_____

_____

_____

_____

_____

_____

_____

_____

_____

I Trust You Lord!

Mem

Oh, how I love Your guidance!
It is my meditation all the day long.
You, through Your path, make me
wiser than all worthless thoughts,
for they are ever with me.
I have more understanding than all
my teachers.
Because Your victories are what I
spend my time thinking about.
Your victories are my meditation.
I understand more than the ancients.
Because I hold on to Your grace and truth.
I restrain my feet from every evil way,
that I may experience Your Word.
I hold on to Your promises on Your path.
All of Your promises are Yes in Christ.
You, Yourself, have taught me

through faith in Your Word, on Your path.
How sweet is Your Word to my taste,
sweeter than honey in my mouth.
Through Your grace and truth I get
understanding. Forever and ever throughout
eternity. I hate every false path, every
false thought, every false way.

911 What Is Your Emergency?

Holy Spirit, today, right now I need...

_____

_____

_____

_____

_____

_____

_____

_____

_____

_____

_____

_____

_____

_____

_____

_____

I Trust You Lord!

911 What Is Your Emergency?

Holy Spirit, today, right now I need...

_____

_____

_____

_____

_____

_____

_____

_____

_____

_____

_____

_____

_____

_____

_____

_____

_____

_____

I Trust You Lord!

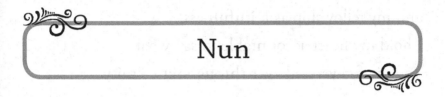

Nun

Lord, Your Word is a lamp to my feet.
A light into Your presence.
Even when I am extremely troubled
I swear and confirm
that I hold onto Your righteous Word.
Breathe into me Lord; restore my soul
according to Your Word.
Lead me in the path of righteousness.
Accept, I pray, the freewill offerings
of my mouth,
Lord, and teach me Your Word!
My life is continually in Your hand.
I move by faith in Your Word.
Wicked thoughts lay a snare for me.
Even so, I do not stray from Your grace and truth.
Your victories I accept as a heritage
forever and ever throughout eternity.

For they are the rejoicing of my heart.
I believe You.
Lord, please account my faith as righteousness
and my fellowship as faithfulness.
I hold my heart accountable to say what
You say forever and ever throughout eternity.

911 What Is Your Emergency?

Holy Spirit, today, right now I need...

_____

_____

_____

_____

_____

_____

_____

_____

_____

_____

_____

_____

_____

_____

_____

_____

_____

I Trust You Lord!

911 What Is Your Emergency?

Holy Spirit, today, right now I need...

_____

_____

_____

_____

_____

_____

_____

_____

_____

_____

_____

_____

_____

_____

_____

_____

_____

_____

I Trust You Lord!

Samek

I hate double-minded thoughts Lord,
but I love walking by faith in Your Word.
Your Word is my hiding place
and my shield from worthless thoughts.
I hope in Your Word.
When thoughts of sorrow and worry
come upon me,
I command them In the name of Jesus,
depart from me
you contrary, troubling thoughts
and be cast into everlasting fire.
For I keep on the path of my God!
Uphold me God according to Your
Word, that I live victoriously.
Do not let me be ashamed of my hope.
Please God!
Hold me up and I am safe from worthless

thoughts. I say what You say continually.
You reject all thoughts who
stray from saying what You say.
For those thoughts are falsehoods.
You put away all wicked thoughts
roaming the earth like trash.
This body You gave me trembles with
obedience to You,
and I reverence Your Word.
Forever and ever throughout eternity
I love Your victories.
Lord, Your Word I hide in my heart
that I not sin against You.
Please help me!
From everlasting to everlasting You are God.

911 What Is Your Emergency?

Holy Spirit, today, right now I need...

_____

_____

_____

_____

_____

_____

_____

_____

_____

_____

_____

_____

_____

_____

_____

_____

_____

_____

_____

I Trust You Lord!

911 What Is Your Emergency?

Holy Spirit, today, right now I need...

_____

_____

_____

_____

_____

_____

_____

_____

_____

_____

_____

_____

_____

_____

_____

_____

I Trust You Lord!

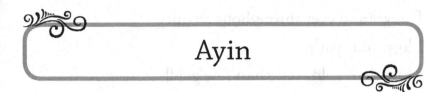

Ayin

I pray for goodness and mercy, faithfulness
and righteousness.
Do not leave me to oppressing thoughts.
Be surety for me for good.
Please Lord, do not let contrary
thoughts oppress me.
My soul weeps reaching for Your
righteous Word and Your deliverance.
Commune with me according to
Your Holy Spirit and teach me how to
say what You say.
I belong to You Lord; open to me
the gates of righteousness and I will
be secure and safe.
Give me understanding,
So that I personally experience Your victories.
Let me not wander from Your path

or Your way.

For worthless thoughts treat faith in

You as powerless.

Forever and ever throughout eternity

I love Your path.

More than gold, yes, than fine gold!

You have taught me that grace and

truth stand supreme in all things.

911 What Is Your Emergency?

Holy Spirit, today, right now I need...

_____

_____

_____

_____

_____

_____

_____

_____

_____

_____

_____

_____

_____

_____

_____

_____

_____

_____

I Trust You Lord!

911 What Is Your Emergency?

Holy Spirit, today, right now I need...

_____

_____

_____

_____

_____

_____

_____

_____

_____

_____

_____

_____

_____

_____

_____

_____

_____

I Trust You Lord!

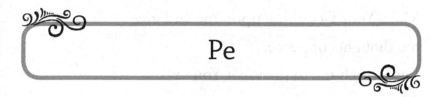

Pe

Your victories Lord are wonderful.
Forever and ever throughout eternity
my soul holds on to them.
From everlasting to everlasting You are God.
The entrance of Your Word gives light.
It gives understanding to the simple.
I open my mouth and pant.
I long for Your path.
Look upon me Lord and guide me in
Your Holy Spirit,
as Your custom is towards those who
love Your name.
Teach me to not listen to thoughts of fear
as You direct my steps, hold my hand, and
help me by Your Word.
And let no oppressing thoughts have
dominion over me.

Declare me strong and keep me constant
from the oppression of worthless thoughts
that I may hold onto Your grace and truth.
Make Your face shine upon me and give
me thoughts of peace.
Lord, teach me to say what You say.
Rivers of water run down from my
eyes when I do not walk in faith,
in Your protection, in Your Word.
For You alone are God, and
You are God alone.

911 What Is Your Emergency?

Holy Spirit, today, right now I need...

_____

_____

_____

_____

_____

_____

_____

_____

_____

_____

_____

_____

_____

_____

_____

_____

I Trust You Lord!

911 What Is Your Emergency?

Holy Spirit, today, right now I need...

_____

_____

_____

_____

_____

_____

_____

_____

_____

_____

_____

_____

_____

_____

_____

_____

_____

I Trust You Lord!

Tsadde

Righteous are You, Lord.

And righteous is Your Word.

Give me Your victories which You

have commanded for my life.

They are righteousness and faithfulness.

My zeal has consumed me.

But I have not forgotten Your Word.

Your Word is very pure.

Forever and ever throughout eternity

I love it.

I carry thoughts of being small and worthless.

Even so, I do not forget that it is in

Your Holy Spirit that I live, I move,

and I have my being.

I do not forget that from everlasting to everlasting You

are God.

I walk in Your grace and truth.

Your righteousness is an everlasting righteousness,
And on Your path is faith.
Thoughts of trouble and anguish want
to overtake me;
however, by faith I am guided.
Lord, the righteousness of Your
victories is from everlasting to everlasting.
Give me understanding and I will live
and relax in You.
Out of the depths of my soul I cry out to you Lord.
"Give me wisdom and I will hold onto her,
And she will watch over me."
I will love her and she will protect me and help me.

911 What Is Your Emergency?

Holy Spirit, today, right now I need...

_____

_____

_____

_____

_____

_____

_____

_____

_____

_____

_____

_____

_____

_____

_____

_____

_____

_____

I Trust You Lord!

911 What Is Your Emergency?

Holy Spirit, today, right now I need...

_____

_____

_____

_____

_____

_____

_____

_____

_____

_____

_____

_____

_____

_____

_____

_____

I Trust You Lord!

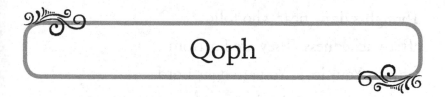

Qoph

I cry out with my whole heart.
Hear me, O Lord!
I will keep saying what You say.
Save me Lord, grant me success.
Send now goodness and mercy to commune
with me.
Declare me strong and constant so
that I walk in Your victories.
I rise before the dawning of the morning.
Out of the depths of my soul I cry for help.
I trust Your Word!
Yes, I do.
My eyes are awake through the hours
of the night.
In the silence of the night I can meditate
in Your Word.
I hear Your voice according to

Your lovingkindness.
Lord, breathe into me, restore my
soul according to Your justice.
Thoughts draw near who follow
after wickedness. They are far from
faith in Your love. You are near Lord.
And Your path is clearly shown.
Concerning Your victories,
I know deep within me that You
have provided them for me forever.
Please surface them in my life.
Please give them to me now!

911 What Is Your Emergency?

Holy Spirit, today, right now I need...

_____

_____

_____

_____

_____

_____

_____

_____

_____

_____

_____

_____

_____

_____

_____

_____

_____

I Trust You Lord!

911 What Is Your Emergency?

Holy Spirit, today, right now I need...

_____

_____

_____

_____

_____

_____

_____

_____

_____

_____

_____

_____

_____

_____

_____

_____

_____

I Trust You Lord!

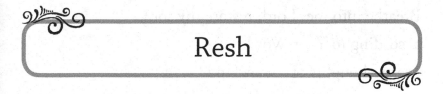

Resh

Lord, consider the worrying and
troubling thoughts who are constantly
confronting me and deliver me.
Now, like never before,
I must remember that I walk by faith,
and not by what seems apparent
wrapped in contrary thoughts.
My mind is fastened on You.
Faith is my substance. Faith is my evidence.
Keep me cradled in thoughts of
perfect peace.
I plead my cause to You and You alone.
Declare me strong and constant
from the oppression of worthless thoughts.
Breathe into me Lord, restore my
soul according to Your Word.
I know that Your deliverance is far

from thoughts of doubt and isolation.

For they do not say what You say.

Great is Your Holy Spirit.

Breathe into me, Lord, restore my soul

according to Your Word.

Many thoughts of sorrow and

worry are my persecutors and my enemies.

Even so, Lord, I watch longingly

for Your victories.

I hear treacherous thoughts and am disgusted.

Because they try to turn me away

from Your Word.

How can I help but sing and shout!

From everlasting to everlasting

You are God.

Consider how I love Your grace and truth.

Breathe into me Lord, restore my

soul according to Your lovingkindness.

The entirety of Your Word is truth.

And Your righteous Word endures forever;

even in my life.

911 What Is Your Emergency?

Holy Spirit, today, right now I need...

_____

_____

_____

_____

_____

_____

_____

_____

_____

_____

_____

_____

_____

_____

_____

_____

I Trust You Lord!

911 What Is Your Emergency?

Holy Spirit, today, right now I need...

_____

_____

_____

_____

_____

_____

_____

_____

_____

_____

_____

_____

_____

_____

_____

I Trust You Lord!

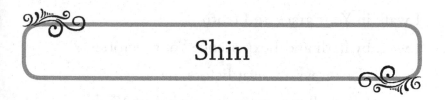

Shin

Now I experience contrary thoughts as
having no power or authority to persecute me.
They are without success.
Because my heart stands in awe of
Your Word.
I rejoice in just the thought of experiencing
Your Word, as one who finds great treasure.
I hate and reject contrary thoughts.
I love walking in Your Holy Spirit.
Several times a day I praise You.
Because righteous are You O Lord,
And righteous is Your Word.
Great peace have those who love
walking by faith in Your Word,
and nothing causes them to stumble.
You have surrounded me with songs
of deliverance. Lord, now my hope is in

restoration as I stay on Your path.

My soul remembers Your victories,

and I love them exceedingly.

I walk in Your grace and truth.

I walk by faith and I experience Your victories.

For all Your ways are ever before me

O Lord, and all my ways are ever before You.

911 What Is Your Emergency?

Holy Spirit, today, right now I need...

_____

_____

_____

_____

_____

_____

_____

_____

_____

_____

_____

_____

_____

_____

_____

_____

_____

_____

I Trust You Lord!

911 What Is Your Emergency?

Holy Spirit, today, right now I need...

_____

_____

_____

_____

_____

_____

_____

_____

_____

_____

_____

_____

_____

_____

_____

_____

_____

I Trust You Lord!

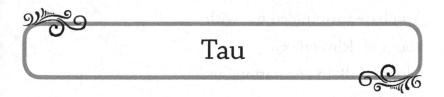

Tau

Lord, let my cry for restoration
continue before You.
Wrap me fully in the understanding
of Your Word, according to Your promise.
Let my prayer of supplication for restoration
continue before You, according to Your Word.
My lips utter praise; I sing and shout!
You are mighty.
You are Holy.
You are omnipotent.
From everlasting to everlasting,
You alone are God.
You have taught me to say what You say.
My tongue speaks of Your Word.
You, O Lord are righteous and Your
Word is righteous.
Your path leads to righteousness

and faithfulness. Your hand, O Lord,
is my help because I hold onto
Your grace and truth.
You have surrounded me with
songs of deliverance.
Now I walk in restoration, and
faith in You is my guide.
Let my soul live, so that it praises You.
Multiply Your Word in me O Lord
to help me. Keep me and guide me,
so that I do not turn from Your path,
from Your Word, from Your way.
It is in Your Holy Spirit that I live,
I move, and I have my being.
From everlasting to everlasting
You alone are God, and You are God alone.

911 What Is Your Emergency?

Holy Spirit, today, right now I need...

_____

_____

_____

_____

_____

_____

_____

_____

_____

_____

_____

_____

_____

_____

_____

_____

_____

I Trust You Lord!

911 What Is Your Emergency?

Holy Spirit, today, right now I need...

_____

_____

_____

_____

_____

_____

_____

_____

_____

_____

_____

_____

_____

_____

_____

_____

I Trust You Lord!

Printed in the United States
By Bookmasters